AF587773

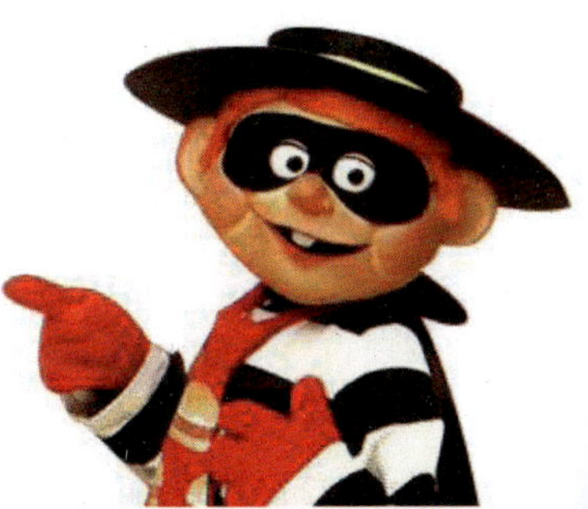

Pilfer (v.): To steal (typically things of relatively little value) [Oxford English Dictionary]

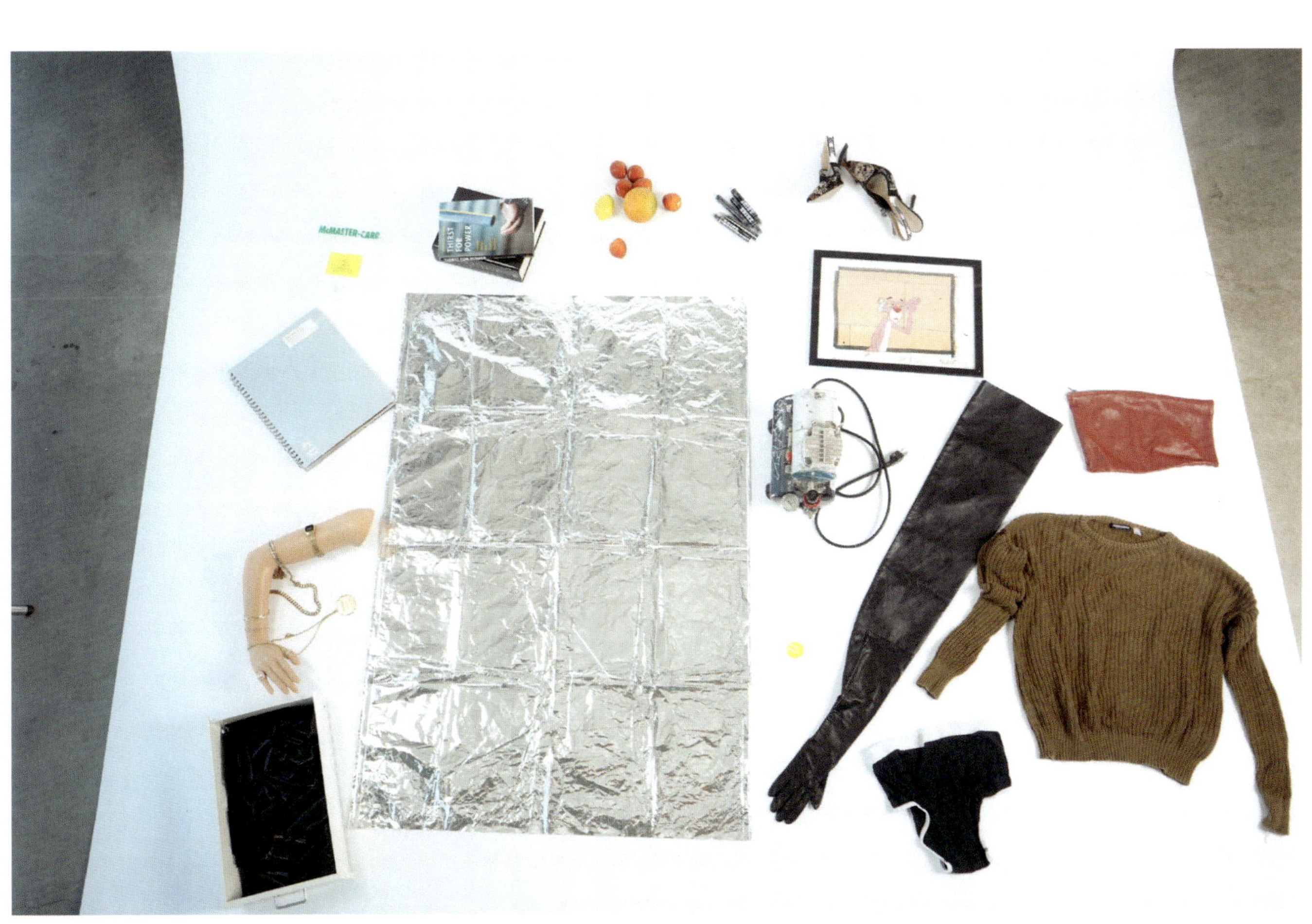
McMASTER-CARR
THIRST FOR POWER

"In a world of thieves, the only final sin is stupidity."

– **Hunter S. Thompson**

Glove

One Glove, 2022

Fabscrap, Brooklyn NY, 2022. Alek Comella

"If you steal from one author, it's plagiarism; if you steal from many, it's research."

– **Wilson Mizner**

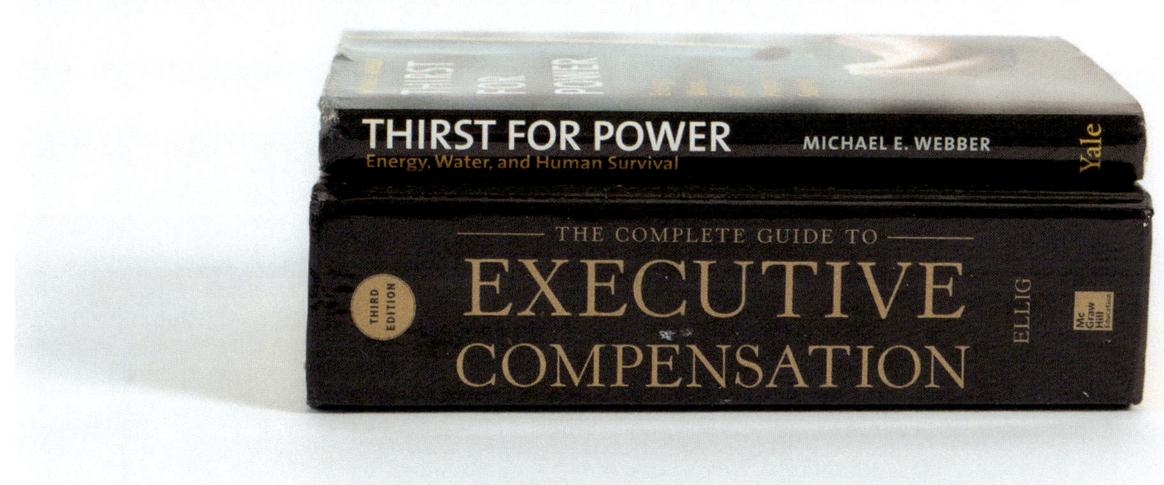

Two Books

Plant Water, 2021

First Republic Bank, Midtown Manhattan, New York NY 2021. Kohlman Harshberger

"You're allowed to steal from Target and also Whole Foods."

\- **Phineas Alexander**

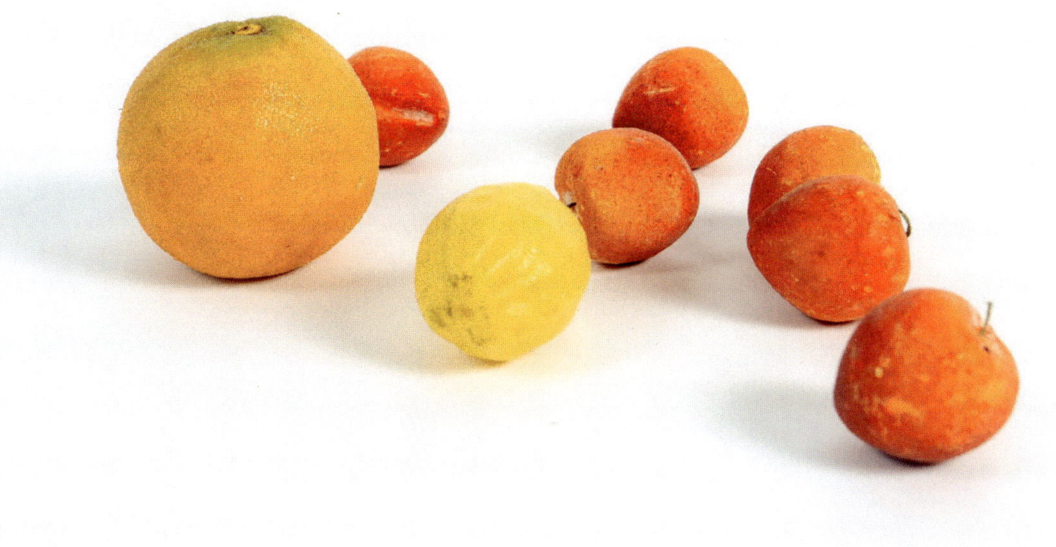

Apples

False Fruit, 2023

New York Studio School, New York NY 2023. Anonymous

"It's not where you take things from – it's where you take them to."

– **Jean Luc-Godard**

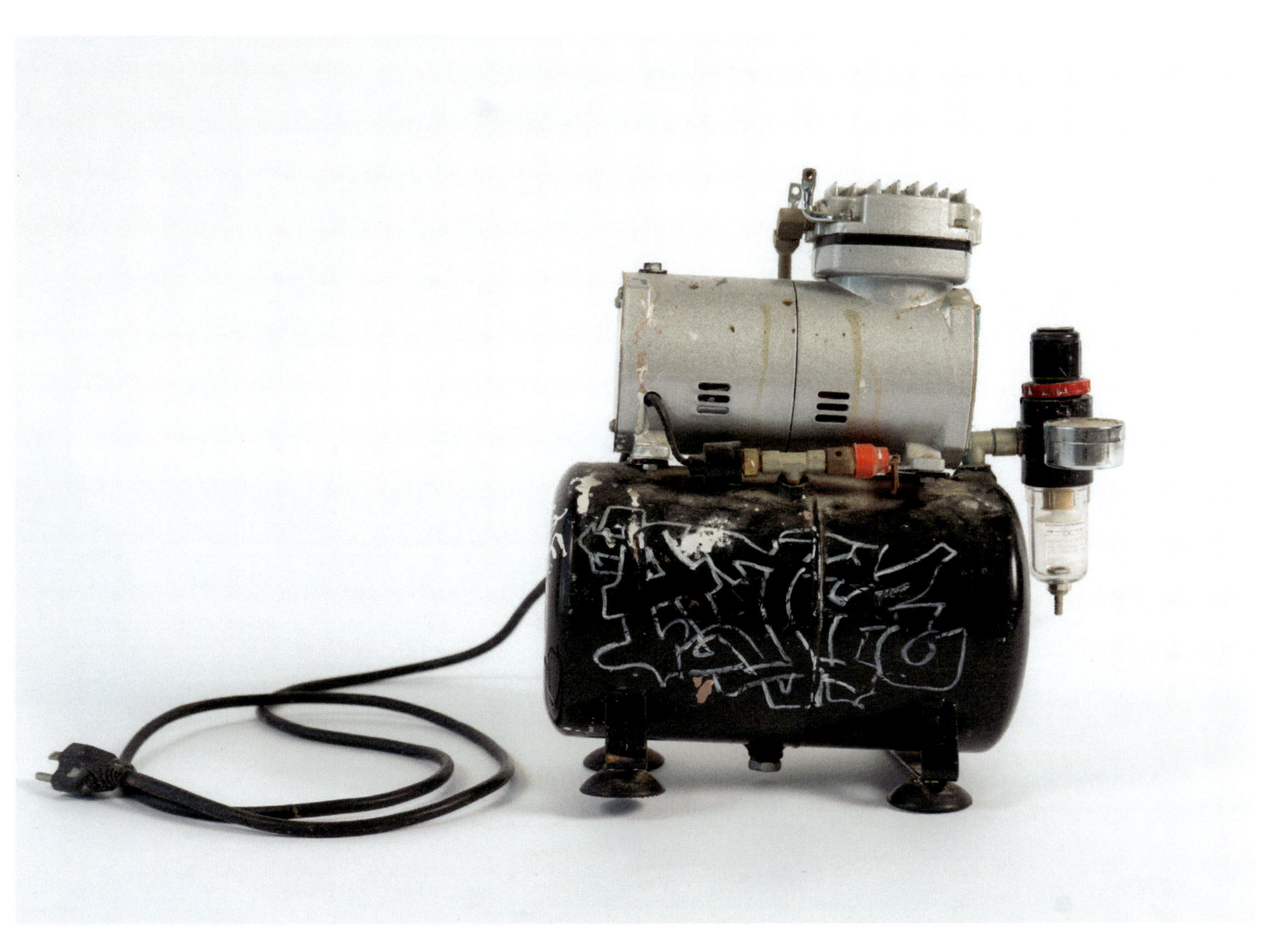

Airbrush

I Broke This Trying to Use it, 2019

The Hole, New York NY. 2019. Anonymous

"One of the surest of tests is the way in which a poet borrows. Immature poets imitate; mature poets steal; bad poets deface what they take, and good poets make it into something better, or at least something different. The good poet welds his theft into a whole of feeling which is unique, utterly different from that from which it was torn."

- T.S. Eliot

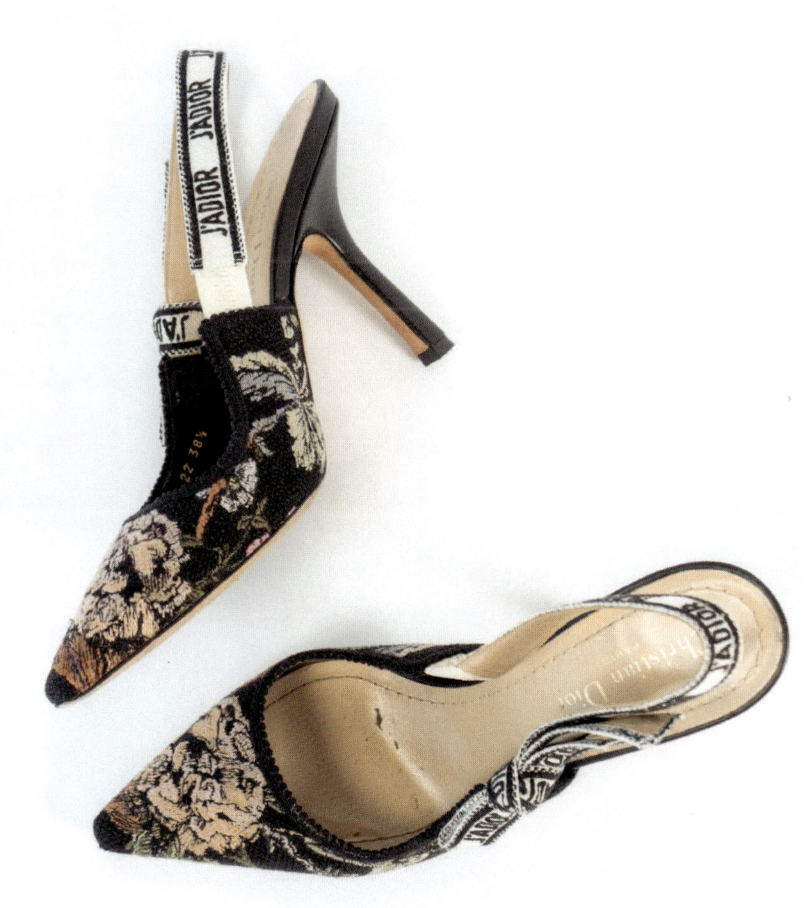

Heels

J'adore, 2024

Dior, New York NY. 2024. Anonymous

"Like Jean Genet, Robert was a terrible thief."

– **Patti Smith**

Matcha

I Can't Think of Anything Smart About a Coffee Chain, 2024

Blue Bottle Coffee Williamsburg, Brooklyn NY. 2024. Danielle Garg

"Does intellectual property count?"

– **Anonymous Submittor**

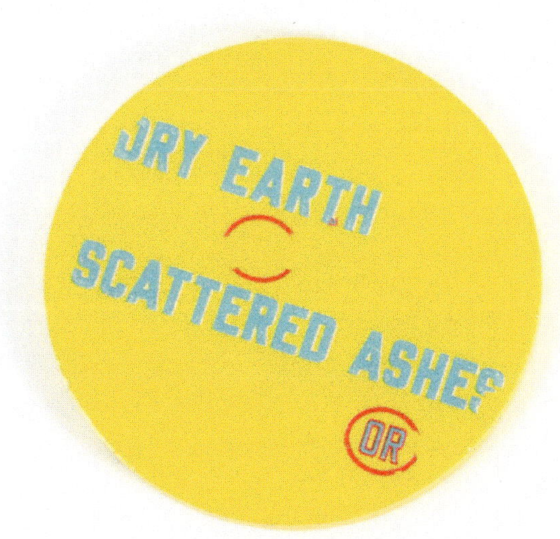

Lawrence Weiner Coin

DRY EARTH & SCATTERED ASHES/DRY EARTH & BURIED GOLD, 2015

Marian Goodman Gallery, New York NY. 2021. Anonymous

"To steal from a brother or sister is evil. To not steal from the institutions that are the pillars of the Pig Empire is equally immoral."

- **Abbie Hoffman**

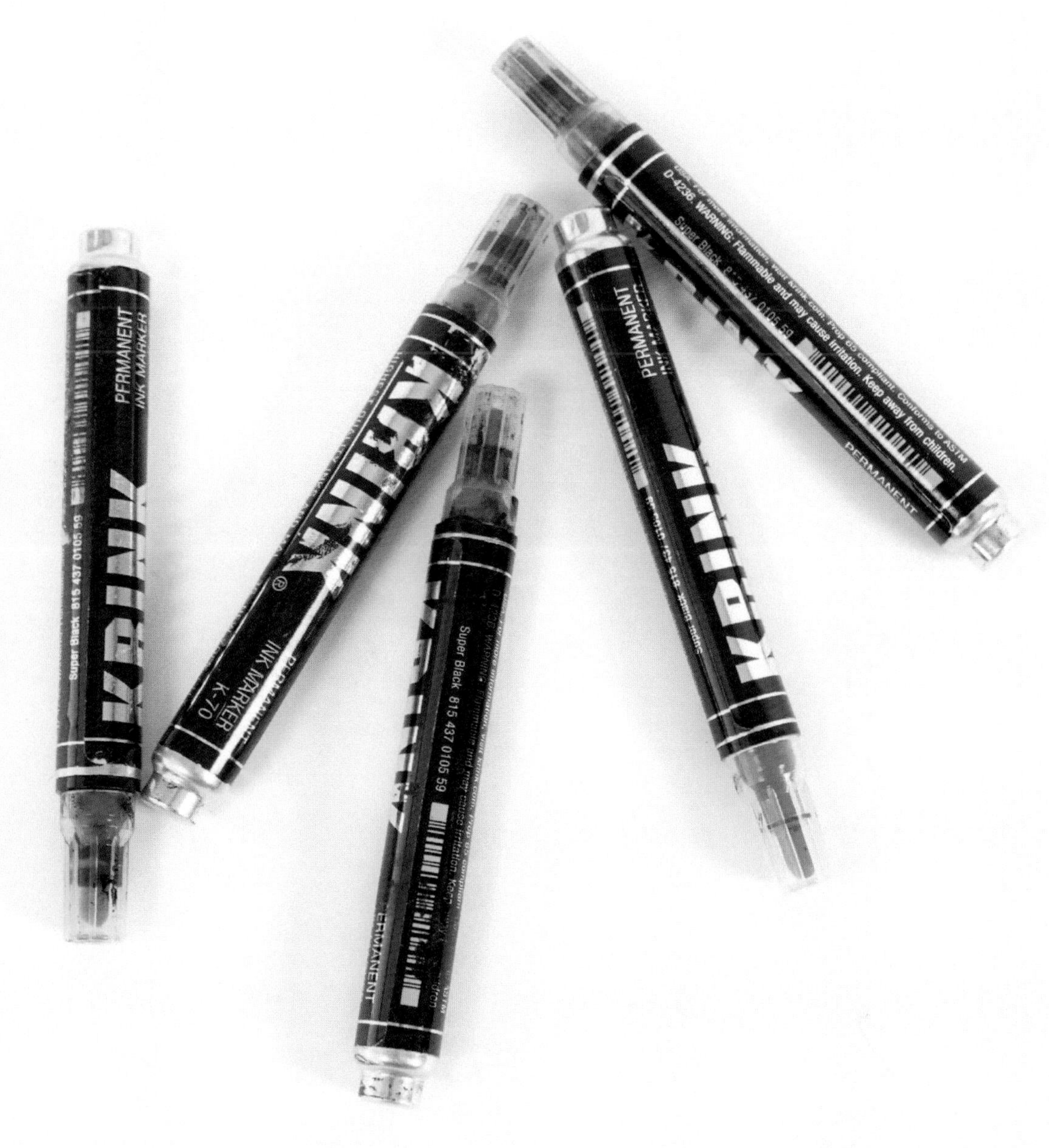

Paint Pens

Used for Tracing, 2024

Tom Sachs Studio, New York NY. 2024. Anonymous

"May your shadow never grow less (or stealing would be too easy!)"

- **J.R.R Tolkien**

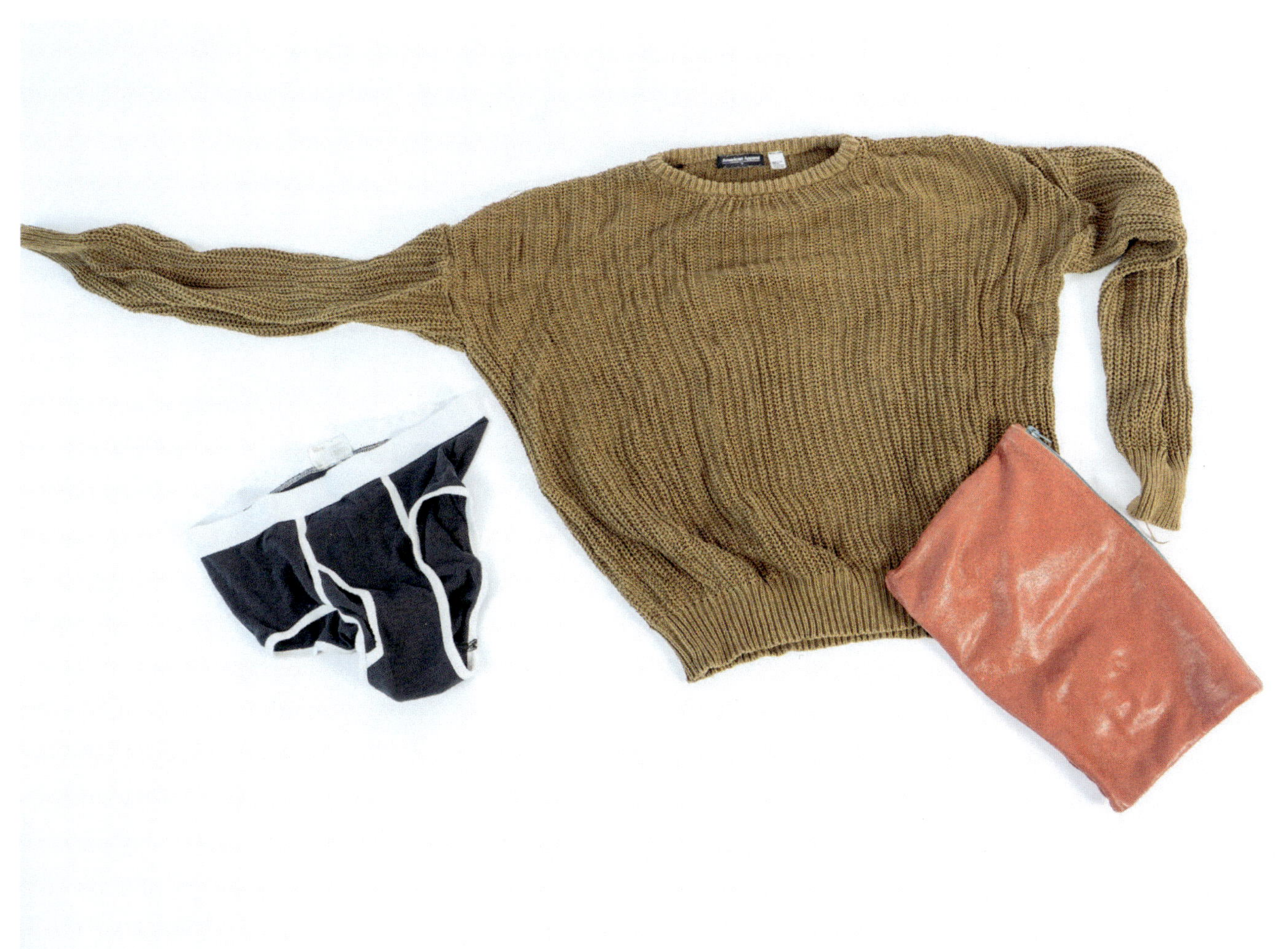

American Apparel

Year Abroad, 2017

American Apparel, Atlanta GA. 2017. Anasha Stevens

"Good name in man and woman,
dear my lord,
Is the immediate jewel of their
souls:
Who steals my purse steals
trash; 'tis something, nothing;
'twas mine, 'tis his, and has
been slave to thousands;
But he that filches from me my
good name
Robs me of that which not
enriches him,
And makes me poor indeed."

- **William Shakespeare**

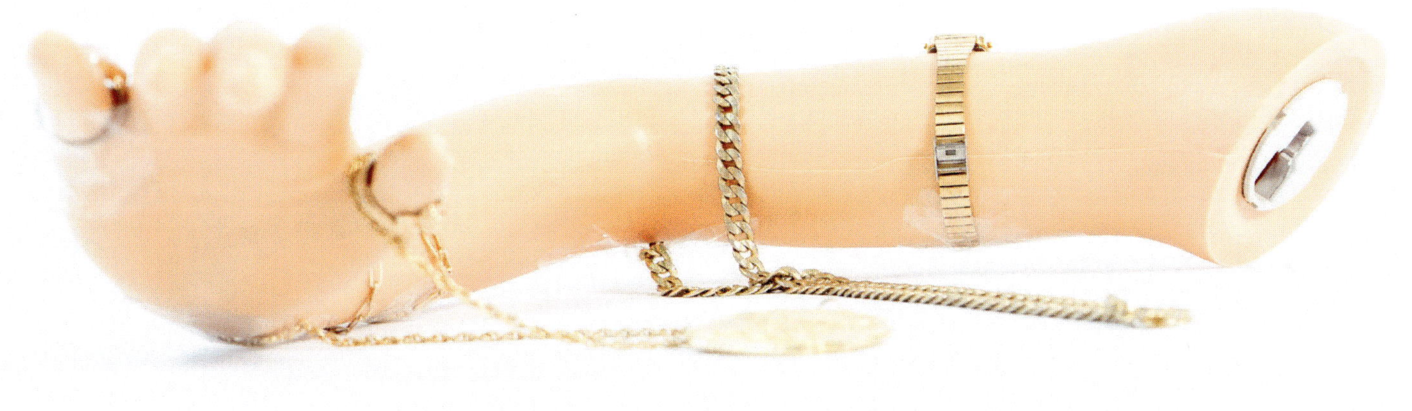

Things People Have Left Behind

Exquisite Corpse, 2024

Necklace 1: Harp and Crown,Philadelphia PA. 2019
Braclets: The Love, Philadelphia PA. 2020
Necklace 2: Standard Hotel, New York NY. 2023
Arm: Ace Bar, New York NY. 2022

Jordan Princiotta, 2019-2023

“The whole reason I worked there was to steal printer ink.”

- Anonymous Submittor

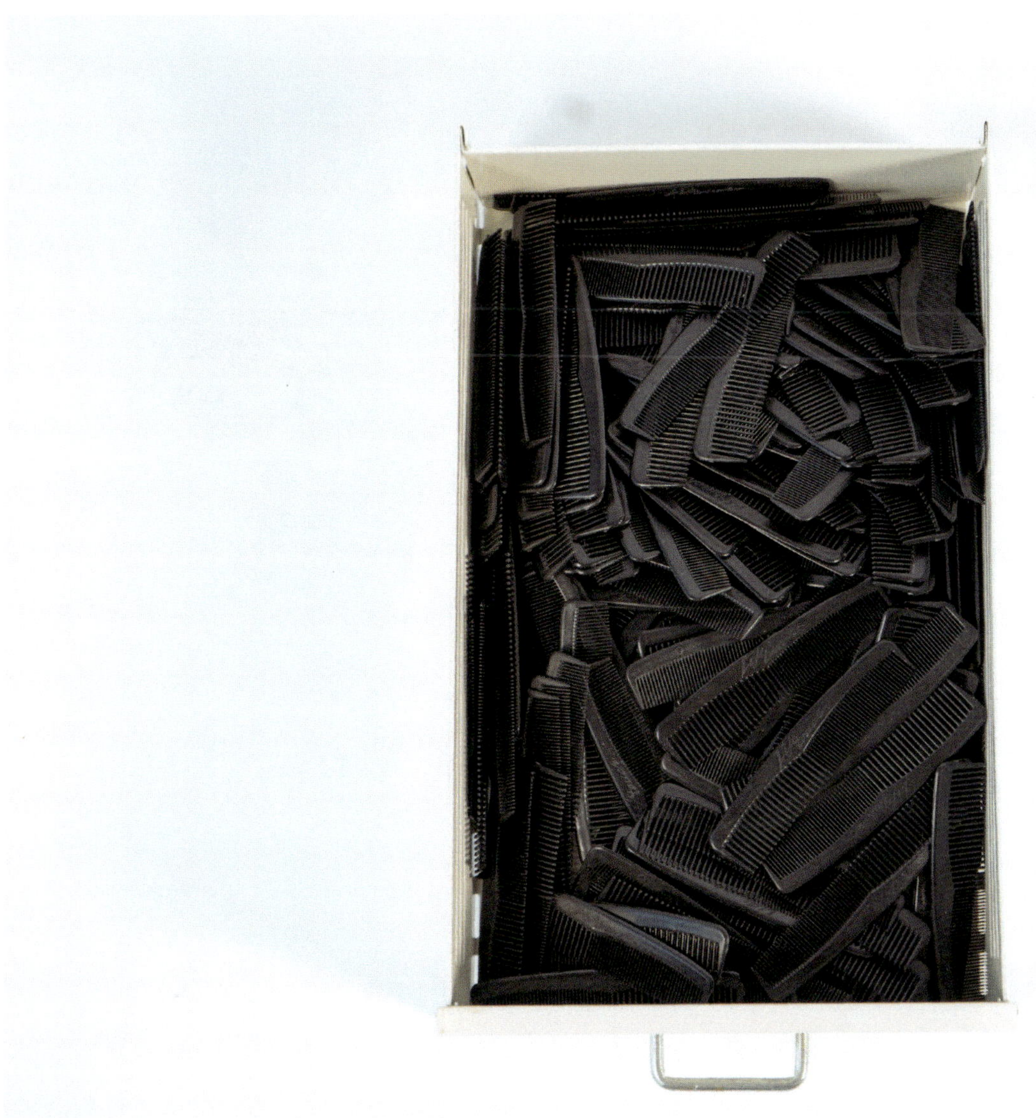

Black Combs

Has Your Employee Been Stealing From Work?, 2024

Lifetouch, Philadelphia PA 2010 Kat Thek

"Better to be poor than a thief, but better to be a thief than starve."

– **Unknown**

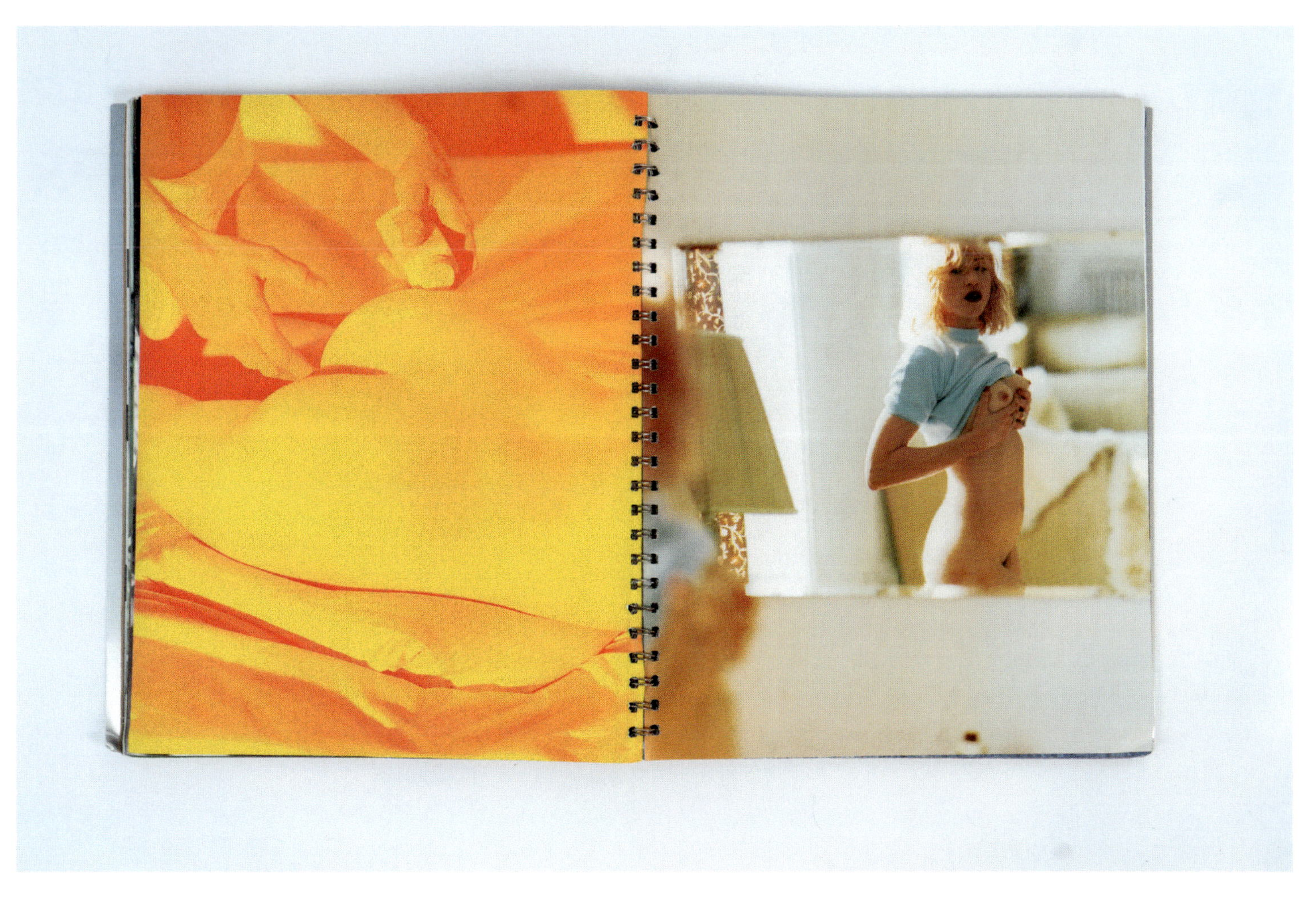

Madonna Sex Book

All That Just to See Madonna Naked, 2024

Haringey Council Library, London, UK. 2022. Tom Coates

"Museums are secular churches . . . and to steal there is blasphemous."

– **Michael Finkel**

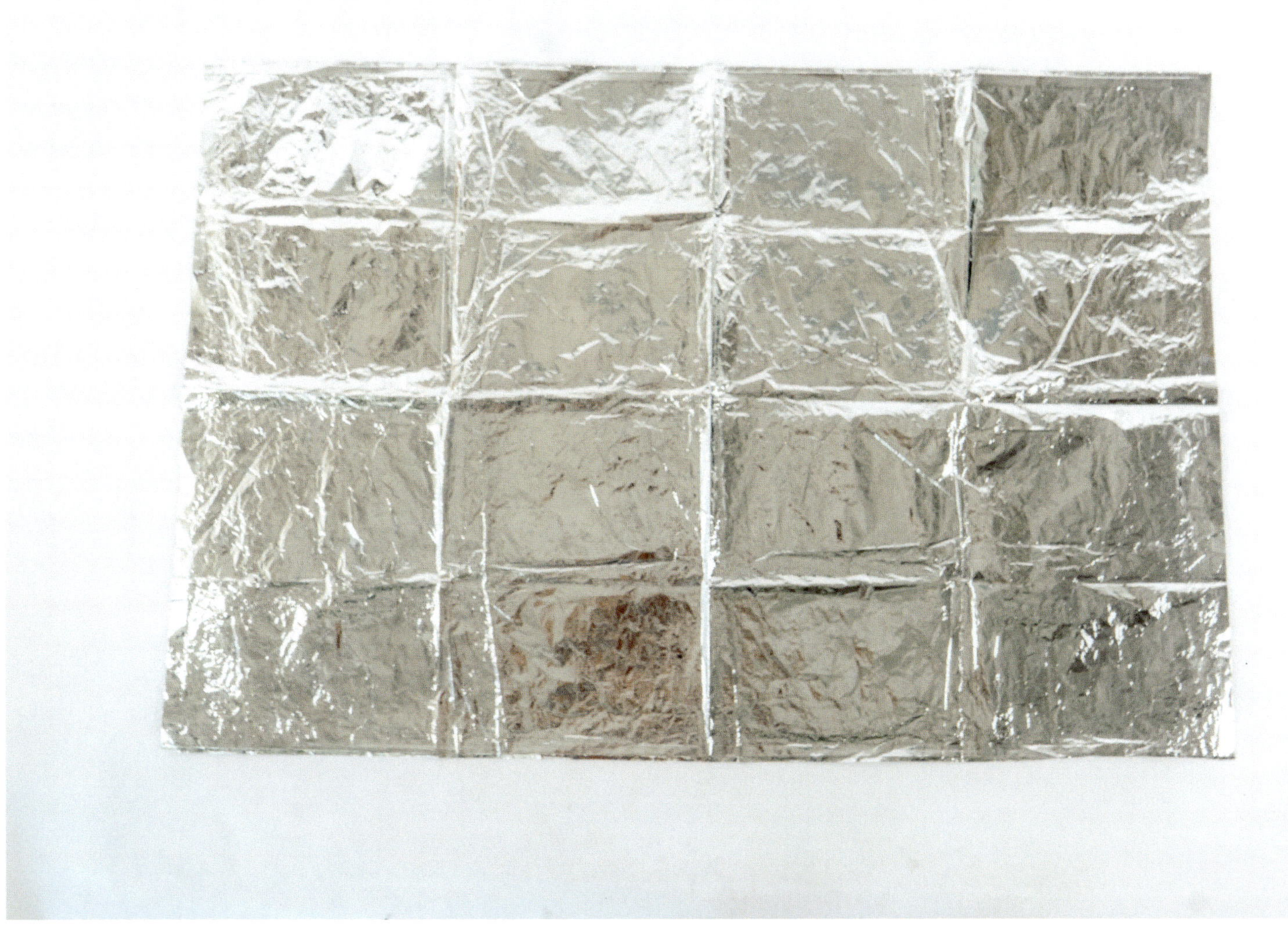

Silver Balloon

Andy's Balloon, 2022

Tate Modern, London UK. 2020. Anonymous

“Good artists copy, great artists steal.”

– **Pablo Picasso, falsely attributed**

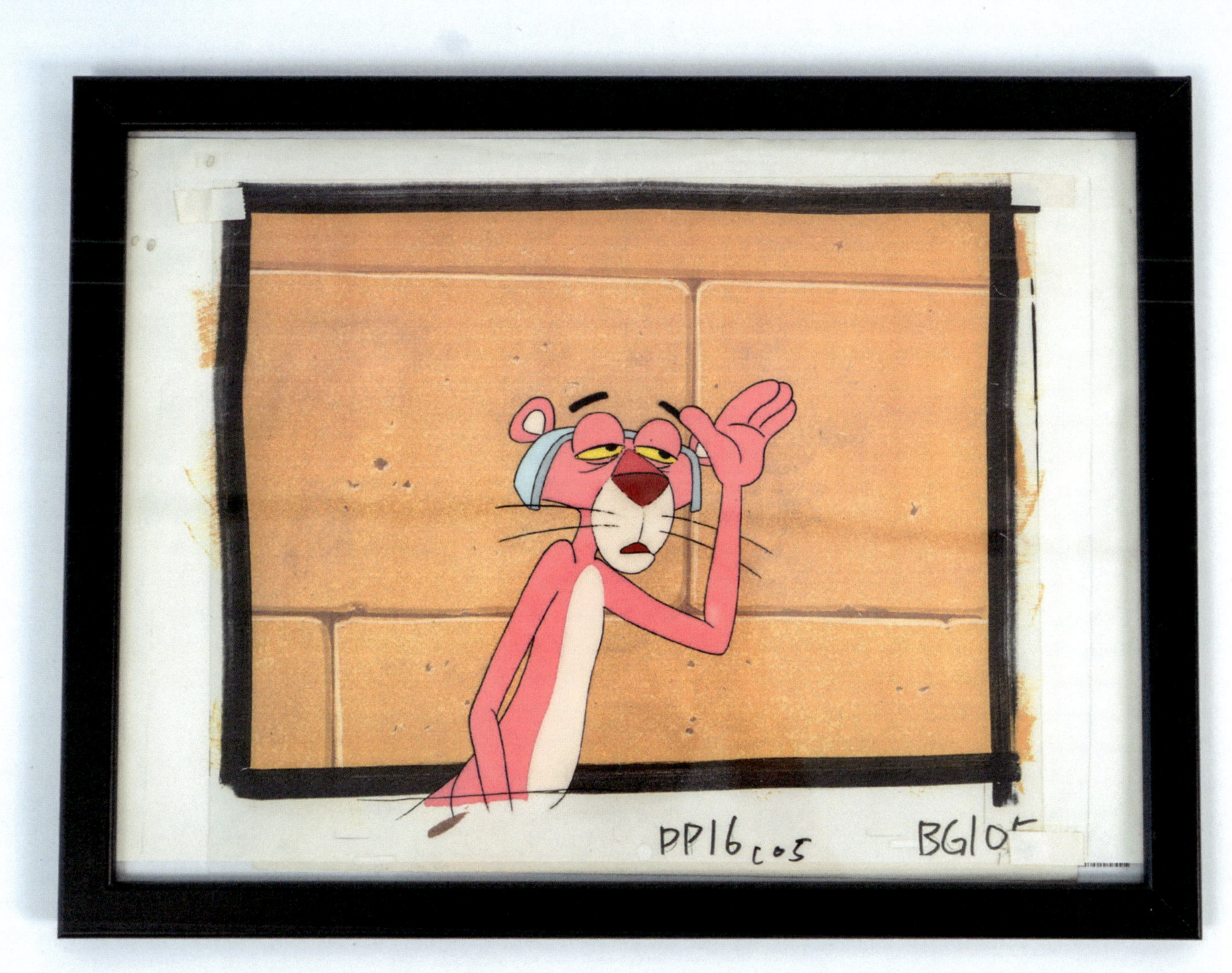

Original Pink Panther Animation Cel

Why Can't Humans Behave More Like Animals?, 2024

Framestore, London UK 2018. Anonymous

"Nothing is original. Steal from anywhere that resonates with inspiration or fuels your imagination. Devour old films, new films, music, books, paintings, photographs, poems, dreams, random conversations, architecture, bridges, street signs, trees, clouds, bodies of water, light and shadows. Select only things to steal from that speak directly to your soul. If you do this, your work (and theft) will be authentic. Authenticity is invaluable; originality is nonexistent."

- **Jim Jarmusch**

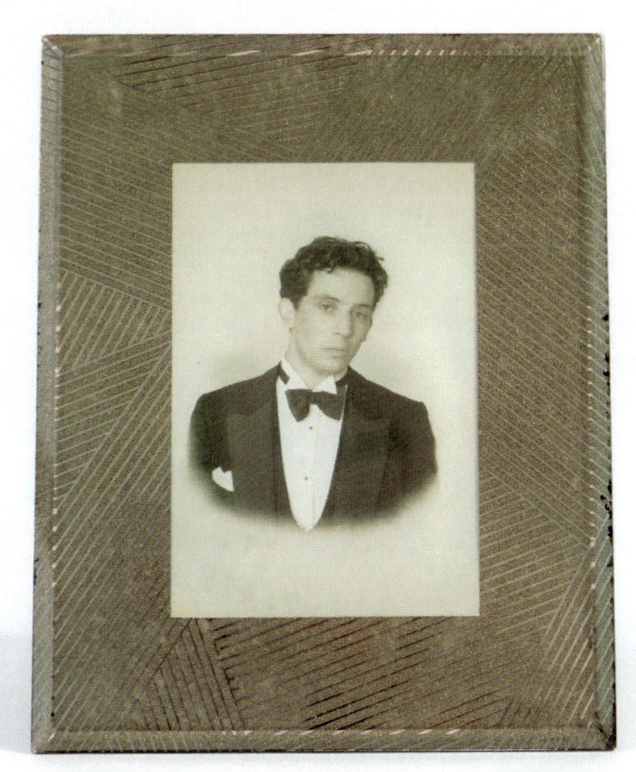

Prince Charles Photo

Josh O'Conner, 2023

Eccentric Trading Company, London UK. 2024. Anonymous

"There's a lot for screenwriters to steal from songwriters, in terms of getting to the point."

– **Paul Thomas Anderson**

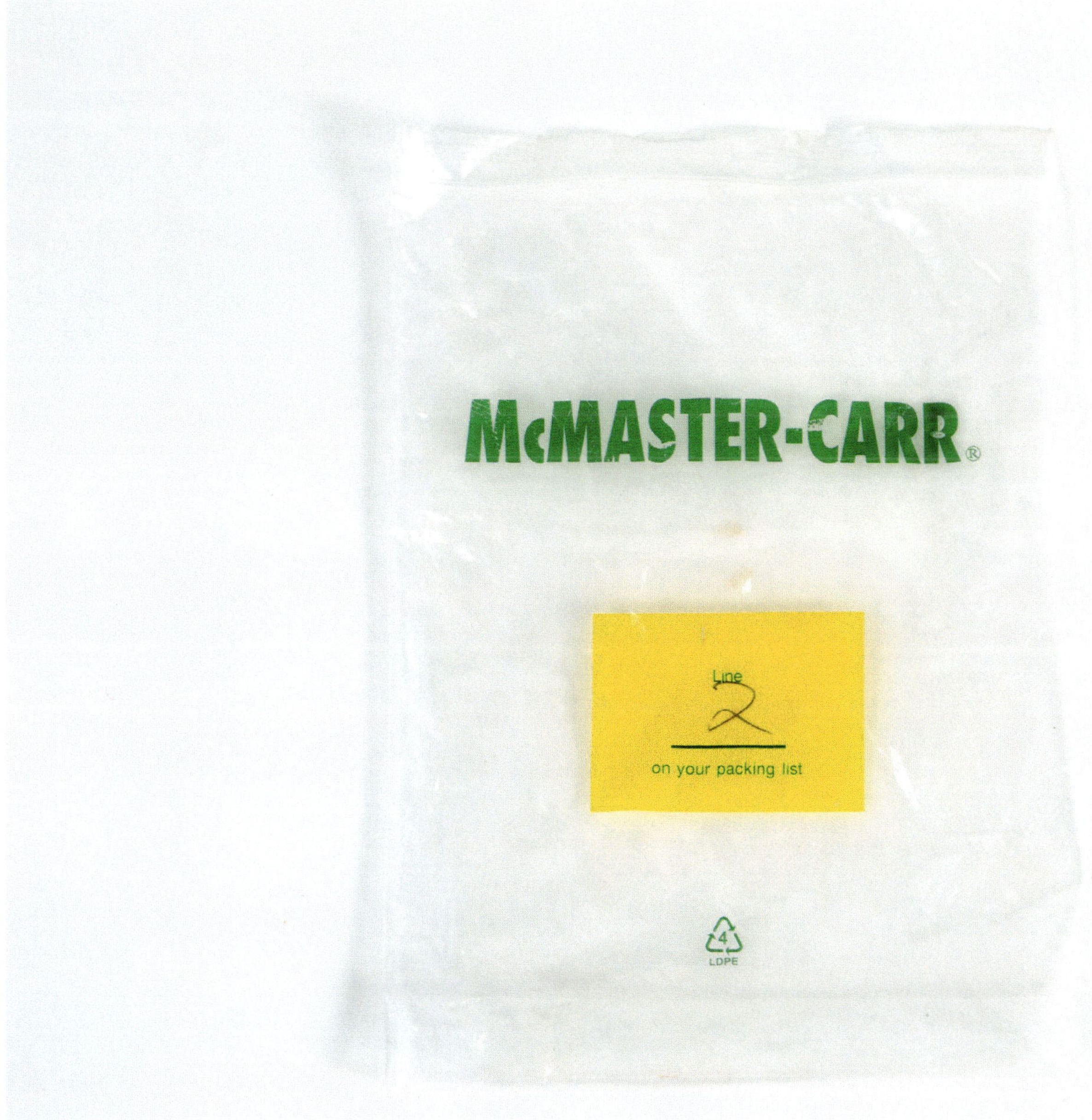

McMaster-Carr Bag

The Amazon of Industrial Parts, 2024

McMaster-Carr, Elmhurst IL, 2023. Aline Ko

“What about time? I’ve stolen time.”

- Anonymous Submittor

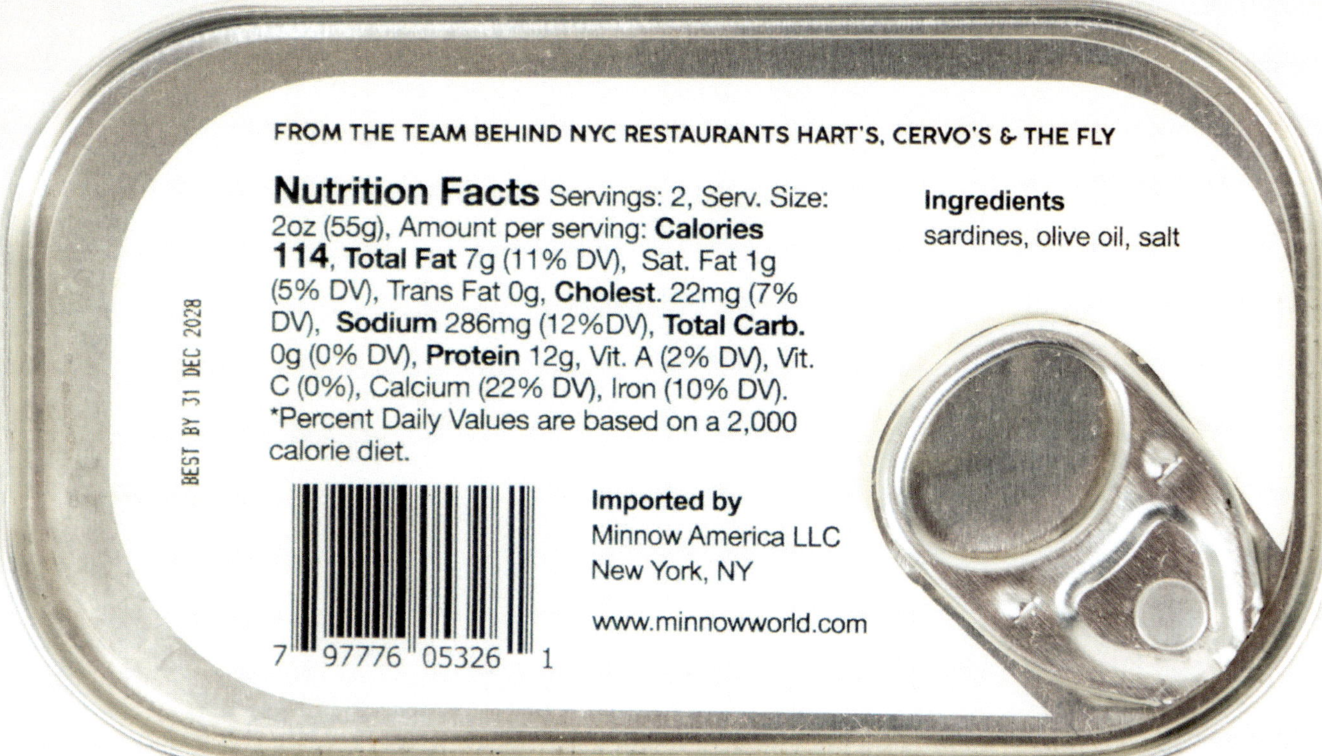

Sardines

Couldn't Include the Chicken, 2024

Cervo's, New York NY, 2024. Anonymous

"Nobody will give you freedom.
You have to take it."

– **Meret Oppenheim**

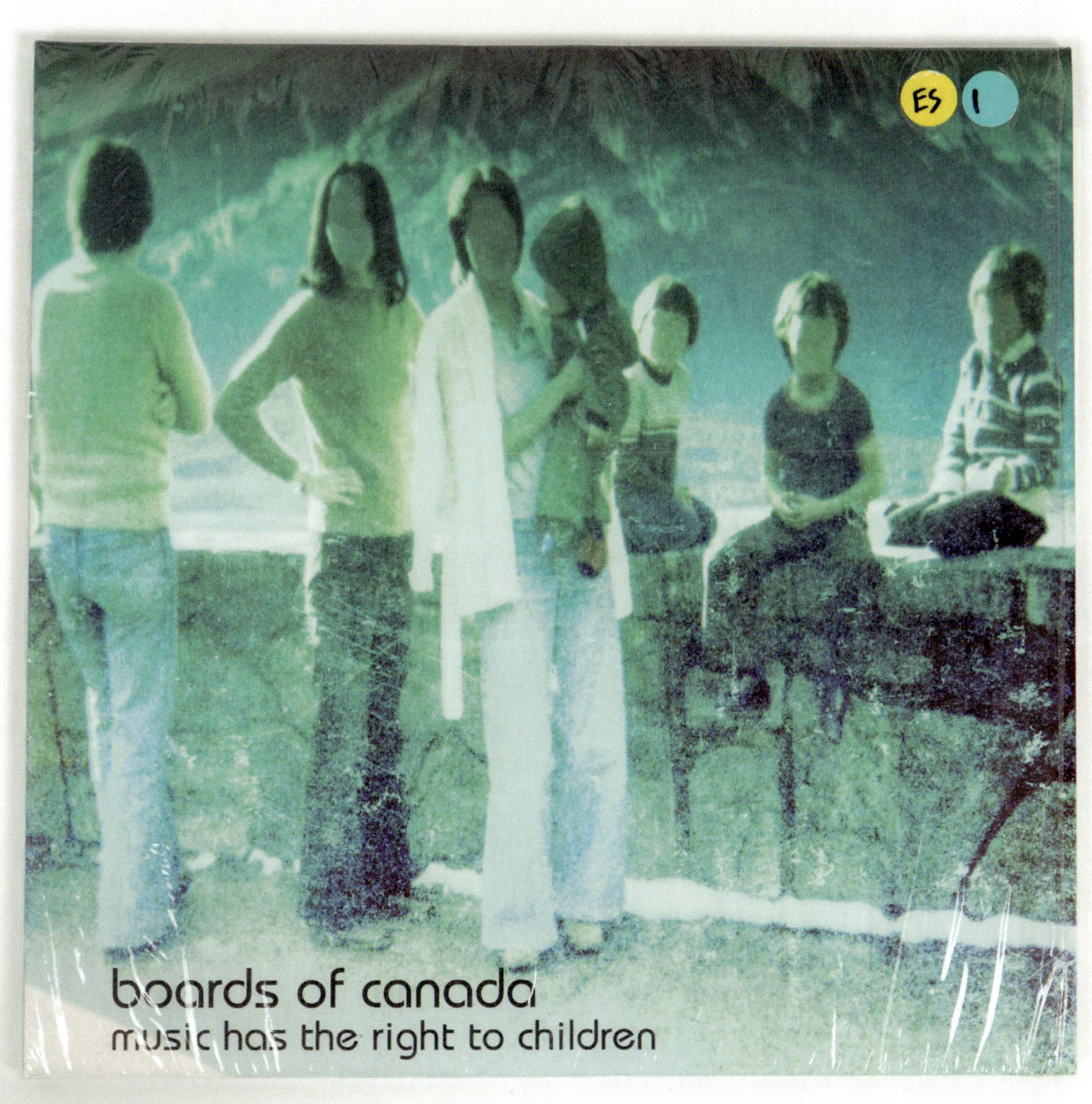

music has the right to children

I Was The Only One Who Would Play This Record Anyway, 2024

Eavesdrop, Brooklyn NY. 2024. Jack Chase

“I actually got caught shoplifting at Bloomingdale’s and I was 15 and I was permanently banned from the store, and then like eight years later, I did like a little holiday campaign for them.”

– **Julia Fox**

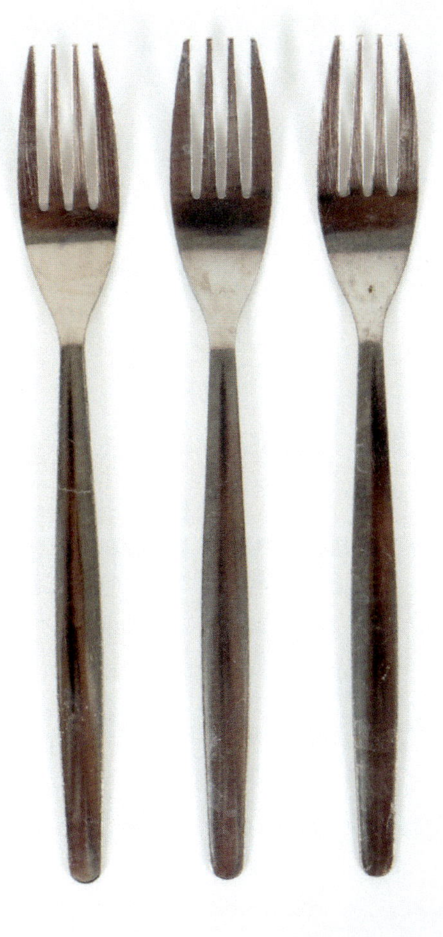

Forks

CITI BANK TRANSFER FROM N.Y TO LONDON, 2024

CitiGroup EMEA Headquaters. Canary Wharf, London UK 2024. Anonymous

"If you want to do a film, steal a camera."

– **Werner Herzog**

When I was a teenager I was paid £60 cash to be a receptionist @ the weekends for the criterion auction house in Angel, London. The man who got me the job was running a racket selling forgeries through the shop and would spend the entire day on a cigarette break. My day consisted of trying to get people to fill out a form as they entered. However I spent it finding the most comfortable and discreet items to sleep on/under. At lunch time I would go and shoplift extravagant meals from the local Tesscos. Occasionally I would do stock checks and help the porter who had no teeth. The best place to sleep was the stock room. There were no cameras and a bed could be made easily. One weekend, I was in the stockroom hiding from my responsibilities. I came across a late 70s Gucci holdall, I began rifling through it. In a zipped compartment I found two plane tickets to somewhere in America, from the early 80s, and a wad of dollars. Knowing full well nobody else knew, and that I was off camera I pocketed the money and shuffled out. I counted it in the toilet and found there was almost 300 dollars. The joy was immense! The next day I travelled to a bank to get it changed The teller claimed it was too old and suggested the post office. They came back with the same response. The money was long out of circulation. I was crest fallen. I kept it for years hoping to find a use for it, or hoping it might accrue some value. Maybe I kept it to remember the story. Anyway I must have given up because I cannot find it.

Robin Finch Pickering –

Robin's Story About Stealing USD

Expired £$, 2024

tolen Dollars, Criterion Auctioners Ltd, London UK, 2016. Robin Finch Pickering

"If you were to include anything I'd stolen, I'd be arrested."

– **Anonymous Submittor**

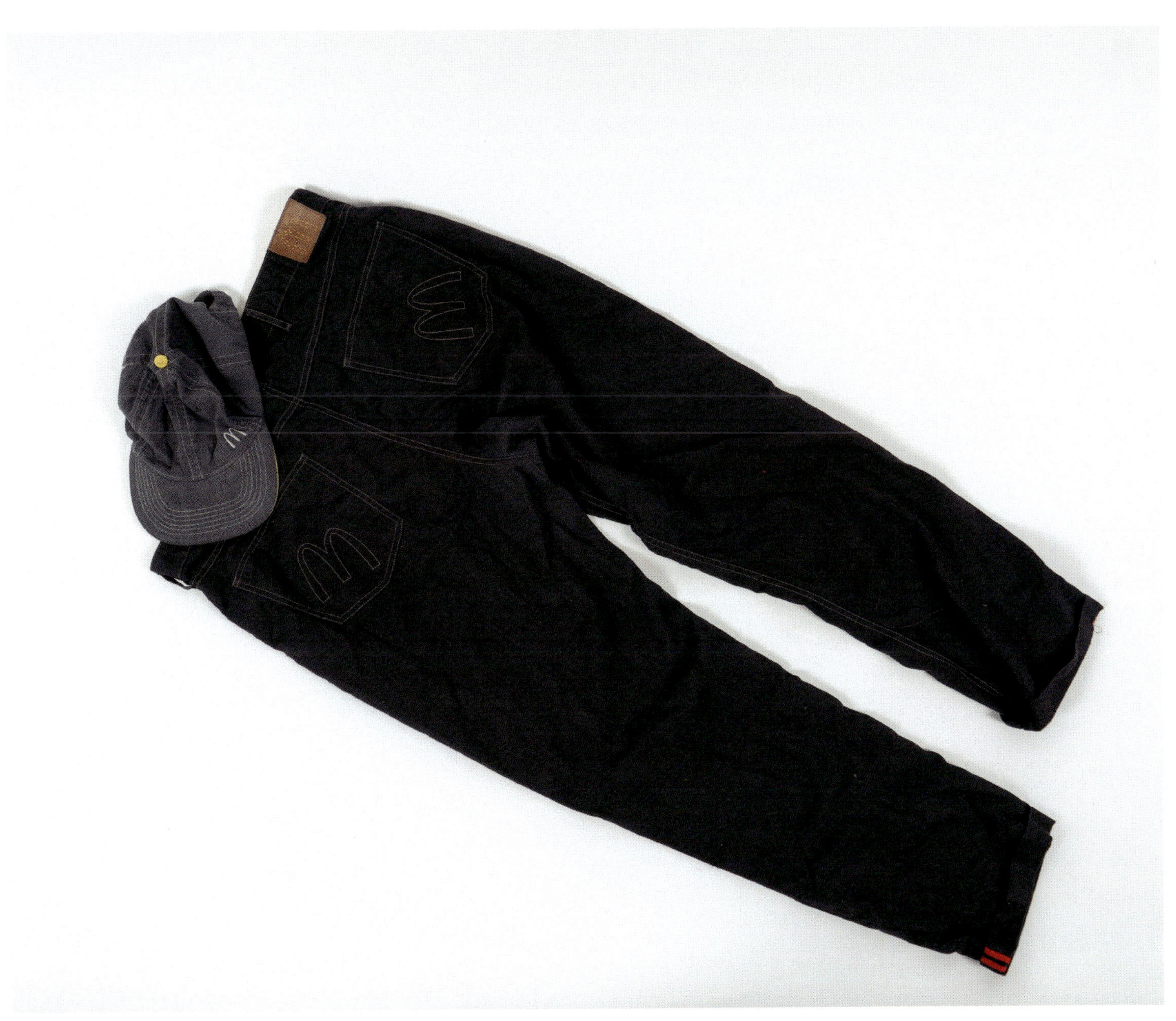

McDonald's Hat and Trousers

Taken Out of Last Paycheck, 2019

McDonald's, Brighton UK, 2019. Emmanuel Odja

"No one earns $100 million. You steal $100 million."

- **Fran Lebowitz**

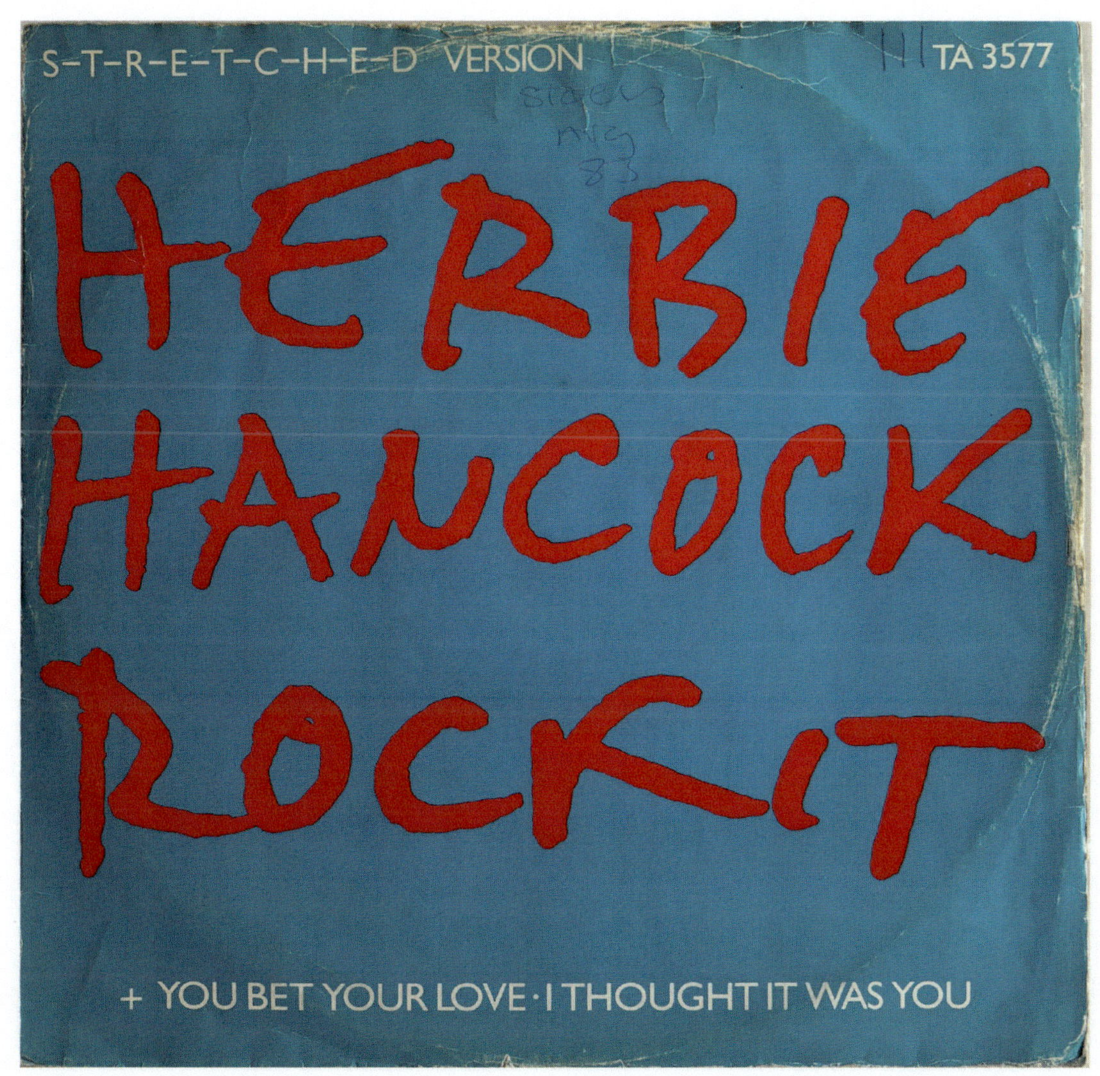

Herbie Hancock Rockit

Rocket - Payback, 2024

Stocks, Kings Road, London UK . 1983. DJ DB

The Show of Stolen Goods, New York City

ISBN: 978-1-963814-14-9

By Jack Chase and Victoria Gill at U-Haul Gallery

Adapted from artist Victoria Gill's London Stolen Goods Show

Catalogue by Jack Chase, Facilitated by Sean Johnson

Organized by Jack Chase, Victoria Gill, James Sundquist

Published by Blurring Books, @BlurringBooksNYC

Special thanks to the contributing thieves.

Number 15 in Blurring Books LSP Series Printed in the U.K. in a CarbonNeutral® facility